GHOSTLY TALES
OF
BRIGHTON'S LANES

To Dee x

Best wishes

Rob Marks

Rob Marks

S.B. Publications

First published in 2010 by S. B. Publications
Tel: 01323 893498
Email: sbpublications@tiscali.co.uk
www.sbpublications.co.uk

Reprinted 2012

ISBN 978-1-85770-357-3

Designed and Typeset by EH Graphics
Email: elizhowe515527@gmail.com   Tel: 07734 923 796

CONTENTS

INTRODUCTION

Greetings, ghost hunters! Are you brave enough to journey with me into the shadowy netherworld twixt this life and the next? If so, then you can consider yourself a true ghost hunter; if not, perhaps you should put down this little volume down right now. For, as the title suggests, all my stories are well documented accounts of unexplained paranormal goings on in and around Brighton's famous *Lanes*.

Many will frequently dismiss the existence of ghosts and seek a logical or scientific explanation for such phenomena. In many instances logical explanations can indeed be found. Ask yourself how often have you imagined things you know aren't really there, or allowed your eyes or ears to play tricks on you, particularly at night? I'm fairly certain we've all done it at one time or another. Yet there also exists a grey area that frequently defies rational understanding. Furthermore, there is a good deal of evidence to suggest that supernatural forces do exist. Certainly tales of ghosts and the spirit world have pervaded virtually every culture for centuries. Moreover, whether one is a believer or not, they will frequently find themselves drawn by tales of the paranormal.

As a child I became captivated by *Algernon Blackwood's Tales of Mystery* on our black and white television and thereafter came to enthuse over all stories of strange and unexplained goings on. The element of mystery and the unknown was extremely appealing, as was the anomaly of taking pleasure in scaring oneself - at least until bedtime arrived! In the swirling darkness of my room, spectres seemed to materialise from every nook and cranny. At which point I generally took a dive beneath the relative safety of my bedclothes.

As the years passed I always maintained a sporadic interest in the supernatural, often dipping into the odd anthology of ghostly tales. Nevertheless, it was only when I began teaching that I became acutely more aware of the skills involved in conceiving and writing a good ghost story and, moreover, the subtle linguistic devices deployed by writers' for hooking the reader and building tension in their stories. I would certainly not profess to be in the same league as the many great writers of this genre. My little yarns are merely adaptations of documented accounts often passed down through generations.

My first active involvement in the supernatural, as a writer and entertainer, came about whilst living in York, which is widely reputed to be Britain's most haunted city. I was dividing my time between teaching drama and theatre studies whilst trying to carve a niche for myself in the world of entertainment. Around this time I became involved with the concept of developing a ghostly show to perform on York cruise boats, which eventually came to be known as the *Ghost Cruise.* Dressed in the garb of an old Victorian ferryman, I soon found myself spinning grisly tales of the paranormal to groups of international tourists as the boat drifted lazily through the city.

I came to realise that ghost stories were an excellent vehicle for entertainment and particularly rewarding to the performer. Such tales offered endless opportunities for building dramatic tension, which I soon started to juxtapose with comic respite, lifting the audience to a gripping high point before making light of the more gruesome elements in the stories with humorous asides.

Having grown up in London I had been visiting Brighton for many years, yet only came to settle there in 2008. By this time I had become immersed in all things ghoulish and so set about researching and developing a ghost walk to perform there. I centred the walk in the old town; more commonly known of as *'The Lanes'.* This small quarter, with its narrow passageways and tightly packed buildings, was once the original fishing settlement of Brighthelmstone; it is the oldest part of the city and, unquestionably, the most haunted. Its quaint myriads of little *twittens* have an old-world appeal offering an excellent backdrop for ghost stories. I soon discovered that, despite the genial ambience in evidence there, lingering reminders of the area's dark past still remained. Many of its former residents were said to lurk in one form or another. In fact there seemed to be

Rob Marks.

scores of haunted locations in this relatively small area.

This pocket compendium offers tourists and locals alike an opportunity to discover these many haunted sites, whilst perusing the accounts associated with them. Drop in for a drink at one of the area's haunted taverns, or take a twilight wander through the haunted gardens of the Old Steine, pay a visit to the old police station at Brighton Town Hall, where a gruesome murder once took place. Alternatively, simply wander the many fascinating twittens; for they all have an absorbing tale to tell. One thing is certain; you will soon discover that there is hardly a street of lane that does not have a spectral connection. Enjoy your ghost hunting!

Rob Marks runs the Ghost walk of the Lanes in Brighton www.ghostwalkbrighton.co.uk

WHISPERING SPIRIT

Little East Street sits in the shadow of Brighton Town Hall and runs from Bartholomews to King's Road on the seafront. Tucked snugly at the southern end is number six, a listed cottage with bow- fronted windows dating from 1800. The building was originally two separate shops; the right half dealing in ironmongery and hardware; the left half a stationers. In the mid-nineteenth century the whole building became a fishing tackle shop under the tenure of Samuel Andrews. It remained with that family up until World War II when it became a tailor's shop. The cottage has since changed hands many times. However, when it became the Strand restaurant in 1997, for some inexplicable reason, paranormal activity began to manifest itself. Many of the staff spoke of hearing their names whispered in their ears. Jim Bingham, the former owner of the Strand, recalled: "My own experiences tended to be hearing my name called from front of house, whilst working in the kitchen during the daytime, walking through into the public area, and finding no one there. This happened to me and others on several occasions throughout my time at the restaurant."

In 2008, a Finnish couple, Pauliina Talvensaan and Manu Leppaney, took over the premises and it became known as Northern Lights; a friendly and welcoming Scandinavian bar. The previous owners had made flippant remarks to them about the building being haunted, but had reassured them there was no cause for alarm as the ghost was quite friendly. Nonetheless, they were somewhat taken aback at the prospect of inheriting a spectral associate with their new business.

Pauliina and Manu were both rational people, and hardly the type to become easily duped into believing implausible tales of ghosts or ghouls. Their rational reasoning was soon to be challenged as they suddenly found themselves wondering if the entity might make itself known; as it turned out, they did not have long to wait.

The staircase leading to the haunted room above Northern Lights. The sounds of footsteps have been heard ascending the stairs.

After much hard work, converting the former restaurant into a bar, an opening night party was held. Copious amounts of Finnish beers and vodkas were consumed and everyone was in good spirits. With the party in full swing the previous owners' accounts of ghostly goings on were all but forgotten. Furthermore, the bar staff remained free of any unearthly mutterings.

At around three in the morning the party came to a close. After the final guests had left, Pauliina and Manu, along with Niklas Vaittien, a member of their bar staff, sat chatting over a quiet drink in the downstairs area. A few minutes later their conversation was unexpectedly interrupted by the distinct sound of footsteps ascending the narrow staircase at the far end of the bar. They each stared at one another in disbelief knowing they were alone in the building. Manu later explained: "It was around 3.00 A.M. and we were having a quiet drink at the far end of the bar. We suddenly heard footsteps going up the stairs, though we knew no one else was in the place. Nevertheless, Niklas and I went upstairs to investigate but found no one." Manu went on to describe the footsteps as "slow and lumbering; the kind one might associate with an elderly or weary person."

It was interesting that the entity had made his presence felt on the opening night. It was almost as if he had been in the bar throughout the whole of the evening's celebrations till finally making his way back to his former room above the bar.

At a later date, whilst on The Ghost Walk of the Lanes', a local psychic paid a visit to number six. At that point he had not been informed of where the spectre had taken to manifesting itself, only that the owners were convinced of an unearthly presence about the place. As he approached the building he became acutely aware of intense paranormal energy emanating from within. On entering the bar the force became even

The haunted upstairs room at Northern Lights.

more overwhelming and led the psychic to recognise two areas giving off paranormal sensations; the staircase and the area around the old fireplace in the upstairs room.

It would make sense that any former resident might take comfort in snuggling beside the hearth on a cold winter's night. However, the psychic was also of the opinion that the bar's ethereal inhabitant was in no way malevolent and was, perhaps, stuck in limbo twixt this life and the next due to a sentimental attachment to his former home.

In May 2009 Pauliina Talvensaan's sister, Anna-Reeta, came to stay and seemed to gain an even deeper insight into the paranormal goings on. Anna-Reeta had always claimed to be spiritually attuned from a very early age and had experienced several paranormal encounters. Moreover, she also professed to have made contact, on a number of occasions, with the 'other side'. Having heard Pauliina and Manu's account of what had happened on the opening night Anna-Reeta was determined to try and communicate with the entity.

Late one evening she sat alone in quiet meditation beside the fireplace in the upstairs room. After a short while she began to attempt contact: "I was in the attic room, sitting close to the chimney. I told of whom I was and who the people were that had moved in. Furthermore, I assured whoever might be listening that these people would look after the house. I then asked that I be given a sign to let me know if anyone was listening. I heard three clear knocks, which seemed to come from the ceiling. As I was trying to establish a connection with the spirit/spirits living in the house the image of an elderly man appeared in my head. From his appearance and gestures I sensed that he was a proud and dignified man who took great pride in his house. Furthermore, that he was intelligent and enjoyed good company and conversation. I also felt he was one who warmed slowly to others, but was reliable once one earned his respect. Nevertheless, I sensed he could, at times, become hot tempered and difficult. My visual image of his appearance was that of a man in nineteenth century gentleman's attire carrying a walking stick or cane."

The sounds of someone pottering around the old fireplace in the upper room at Northern Lights have been heard.

Anna-Reeta also received images of someone else she sensed had lived in the building and, for reasons unbeknown, was being very secretive as she went on to explain: "In the cellar lives a girl who is shy and quiet and who wears a light coloured dress; she is hiding something. Sometimes she walks elsewhere, but she can be felt most in the cellar. When I was trying to reach her, images flooded into my mind of Brighton when there were horses and carriages on the streets and clothes looked very different. The town looked different also, yet I could still recognise it as Brighton. Northern Lights looked different but recognisable."

Whatever the reason for the spirit's presence he has now been adopted by the owners, who see him as a friend and a good spirit. They feel he has made them welcome and given their business his blessing. For this reason they have named their house speciality – a little vodka shot - in his honour and have called it 'Fisherman's Friend'.

Pauliina Talvensaan and Manu Leppänen, the owners of Northern Lights, were disturbed by the sounds of footsteps ascending the stairs whilst alone in the bar.

THE WANDERING NUN

Of all the ghostly legends associated with the Lanes this is perhaps the most tragic. It is the tale of a young nun whose spirit is said to wander one particular little twitten in search of her lost love.

In the twelfth century the Priory of St. Bartholomew stood close to where the Town Hall is today. Legend has it that a young nun lived and carried out various duties there, until the sanctity of her vows was broken by a romantic dalliance with a soldier.

Due to the number of pillaging pirates in those days a detachment of soldiers was sent to protect the priory. The young nun soon fell in love with a handsome soldier of the guard and the couple decided to elope. One night, under the cloak of darkness, and indifferent to the seriousness of their crime, the two lovers crept stealthily away. This was a most serious felony for them both. Any soldier found to have deserted his post in those days would have been hanged. Likewise a nun, running off with soldier, would no doubt have suffered a similar fate. Sadly, the two lovers were soon apprehended and the solder was hanged for his desertion. The fate of the nun, however, was to be one of unimaginable horror and suffering. Nuns and monks who transgressed in those days were often walled up in a tiny space in the cellars of the priory of convent to die from suffocation. In this way the senior ecclesiastics would not have blood on their hands. Her wails and moans must have been heard long into the night as the walls of her tomb grew ever higher. Finally, as the final stone was sealed into place, the poor woman was left to her certain fate.

Her troubled and meandering spirit has been witnessed on numerous occasions, generally on route from Brighton Place to Meeting House Lane, where she has been seen to disappear through a bricked-up doorway to the rear of the Friends' Meeting House.

The bricked-up doorway in Meeting House Lane. The shadowy figure of a ghostly nun has been seen to pass through the doorway.

There is a common myth that this was where she was walled up and left to die. This seems unlikely for two reasons. Firstly, the bricked up doorway is far removed from where the priory used to stand. Secondly, the wall was built several hundred years later. Many believe it is not the ghost of the nun at all, but that of a nineteenth century Quaker woman dressed in a grey shroud who, for reasons unbeknown, haunts the grounds of the Friends' Meeting House.

There have also been other sightings of her restless spirit outside of Meeting House Lane. Some claim to have seen her drifting down the narrow twitten of Black Lion Lane, which runs between the Cricketers and the Black Lion. Certainly, in recent times, the indistinct figure of a woman has been seen drifting eerily between the toilets and the stockroom to the rear of the Cricketers.

The first documented sighting of the nun, however, was during WWII at the time of a blackout. The incident occurred late into the evening when a lady fire watch warden was doing her rounds. On entering Meeting House Lane she was suddenly taken aback at the sight of a woman, dressed in a cowl, who seemed to drift down the passageway before disappearing through the bricked-up doorway. More recently, a couple found themselves engulfed in a most unnatural cold pocket of air close to the doorway. To their astonishment a vague mist began to emanate around the wall. The coiling vapour seemed momentarily to take on human form before drifting silently through the brick-up doorway.

There is still much controversy within the ghost-hunting fraternity as to why she disappears at this particular spot. One such theory is that this could have been the place where she arranged to meet her lover, and that her troubled sprit still returns in the forlorn hope of them being reunited.

Rooms above Dr. Brighton's where poltergeist activity occurred.

1750 in the rendering at Dr. Brighton's

WANDERING APPARITION AT DR. BRIGHTON'S

Visit Dr. Brighton's website and you will be greeted with the following message: "Brighton's premier venue welcoming gay men, women and their friends. We look forward to seeing you soon! Go on, darlin', treat yourself." Need I say more?

Dr. Brighton's is a pleasant, relaxed and inviting pub; whatever one's leanings. It faces the seafront on the corner of Little East Street and King's Road. The building dates from 1750, which can be clearly seen in the rendering above the side entrance.

The pub only acquired its present name in the early nineteen eighties. For many years it had been the Star and Garter Hotel; a modest establishment with some ten bedrooms. The name Dr. Brighton's actually derives out of a character from a novel by William Makepeace Thackeray's titled 'The Newcomes: Memoirs of a Most Respectable Family'. Many years ago, a former landlord decided to adopt this name and had hung a board outside proclaiming "Dr. Brighton's cures and remedies". Needless to say

Dr. Brighton's

the board consisted of a rather extensive list of alcoholic beverage!

Down the years, many customers in the pub, and former hotel guests, have claimed to feel an uneasy presence about the place and, moreover, the feeling of someone watching over them. There have also been many disturbing sightings of shadowy figures and the alarming manifestation of poltergeist activity in an upstairs room.

A shadowy figure has been seen reflected in the mirror above the basin in the gents' toilets, which are housed in the old cellars at Dr. Brighton's.

During the early 1980's, whilst still a hotel, a live-in barmaid had quite a shock one night as she and her boyfriend sat chatting in her room. The young lady in question had, against house rules, smuggled her boyfriend upstairs. The pleasure of being alone in each other's company was soon disturbed by an extremely unsettling incident. As they chatted a strange and unexplained thing occurred. Whilst standing beside her bed the young barmaid suddenly felt a peculiar vibrating sensation beneath her feet. The couple stared at each other, sharing the same puzzled expression. In that instant, cosmetics and ornaments suddenly began to fly from the dressing table. At that same moment a sharp cracking noise was heard and a long split appeared across the full length of the wall mirror.

A sceptic might attribute such incidents to vibration caused by traffic, subsidence or from building work being carried out. The likelihood of heavy traffic causing vibrations strong enough to send items flying from the dressing table would have been most unlikely, if not impossible. Furthermore, no building work was being undertaken at that time, nor had there been any evidence of serious subsidence to the building. What happened next, however, seemed to substantiate this as genuine paranormal phenomena.

The barmaid and her boyfriend were about to begin tidying up when they felt an overwhelming presence about the place. They then noticed an indentation begin to appear in an old armchair in one corner of the room. A vague figure began to emerge, which lasted but a few seconds before beginning to fade.

Unearthly intrusions have also been felt in the gents' toilets, which are housed in the old cellars. Several customers have claimed to see a shadowy figure reflected in the mirror above the basin, but on turning around have found themselves to be quite alone.

It is often said that animals have ESP (Extra-Sensory Perception) and are more attuned to paranormal activity. A former landlord's cat often behaved in a most bizarre manner, frequently spitting and hackling its fur at something it appeared to see in one corner of the bar; though nothing was ever there. A local window cleaner then made a curious discovery in the same area. He informed the landlord how he frequently had to remove what appeared to be the small handprints of a child from a lower pane of glass on the door at the seafront entrance. This was most odd as no children lived on the premises nor were any ever allowed in the bar area.

It was not long after these incidents had occurred that some rather sordid events, relating to the pub's history, came to light. Many years ago, it was claimed, a former landlord had carried out illegal abortions in a room at the top of the building and in the cellars. It was there, more than a century ago, that the tragic death of a young woman and a small child occurred. By all accounts the child was the son of a poor woman who had been left to recover following her crude termination. The child had apparently slipped and become seriously concussed. Weak from her ordeal his mother was unable to come to his aid and, as a result, the child was left to die. It is also believed that the woman never recovered from her termination and also died. In the light of this revelation it is widely believed to be their troubled spirits that meander the building to this day; possibly distraught at their sad and untimely demise.

Inner door at Dr. Brighton's where the small handprints of a child have been witnessed.

THE MANIFESTATION OF MARIA

Maria Fitzherbert was born Maria Anne Smythe on 26th July, 1756. At the age of nineteen she became married to a wealthy land owner named Edward Weld, some sixteen years her senior. Sadly, Edward was killed just three months after their wedding in a riding accident. Three years later Maria married for a second time to Thomas Fitzherbert, but was again widowed in 1781. Due to her inheritance she became a woman of substance and acquired a grand house in Mayfair. It was not long before she began mixing with London high society, where she first became acquainted with George, Prince of Wales.

The prince's attraction to the young widow was instant and a long-standing relationship ensued. He actually married her in a secret ceremony in 1785. However, as he did not have his father's consent, the marriage was not recognised under the Royal Marriage Act. Nevertheless, Maria remained his unofficial wife. In 1804 he instructed his architect, William Porden, to build Steine House. The site overlooking the Old Steine was inevitably chosen for its convenient proximity to the Royal Pavilion. It is in fact widely believed a tunnel was made running between the two buildings to enable

Plaque outside Steine House where Maria Fitzherbert's home overlooking Steine, now the YMCA.

discreet liaisons between Maria and the prince. A bricked-up archway certainly exists in the basement of the building.

Maria had a great fondness for Steine House and remained there until her death in 1837. It seems that her spirit may well have formed a sentimental attachment to the place for the spectral figure of a woman, fitting her description, has been seen there on a number of occasions.

The building has, for many years, been occupied by the YMCA. The majority of those who pass through would probably be quite unaware of its history, which makes one particular sighting all the more interesting.

Steine House; Maria Fitzherbert's former home designed by the architect William Porden in 1801 under the instruction of the Prince Regent.

In 2008 someone claimed they had seen the apparition of a woman in the basement wearing a rather grand dress with hair resembling that of a judge's wig. When showed a picture of Maria Fitzherbert they were convinced it had been her. A similar incident occurred in the spring of 2009, again in the basement area. A young lady employee was startled to see a colleague come running from the lower floor looking shocked and rather short of breath as if he'd been running. When she asked him the matter he explained how he had seen a woman in a long flowing dress drift across the corridor and pass through the wall. The young woman listened with keen interest for she knew the house had once belonged to Maria Fitzherbert. Furthermore, she was aware of similar incidents having been reported down the years. That evening she looked over images of Maria on the internet, printing off a couple to show her colleague the following day. On seeing the pictures he became instantly awestruck. The image of the woman in the picture accurately resembled the drifting apparition he had seen the previous day. Something then occurred to his colleague. She wondered if any evidence of his encounter would show up on the closed circuit video recording and so decided to re-run the tape. What she saw certainly added legitimacy to her colleague's sequence of events. She witnessed him clearly enter the corridor before stopping dead in his tracks, as if he had been startled or confronted by something. He then turned and began running in the direction of the staircase which led to the upper floor. Unsurprisingly, she could see no evidence of the apparition on the tape. This would not have been unusual as paranormal sightings are often only witnessed by individuals at the time; particularly those more attuned to the paranormal.

Around the same time a psychic, while on the Ghost Walk of the Lanes, claimed to feel intense paranormal energy emanating from the lower part of the house. Furthermore, a clairvoyant, who had explored the building, also sensed extreme paranormal activity about the place. The energy had been concentrated around the area of the bricked-up archway where the sightings had occurred. The clairvoyant also sensed a strong male presence in the building. He was further convinced that the spirits of Maria and the prince still resided in the house. As they had shared so much happiness there throughout their lifetimes it would be hardly surprising that their spirits showed a reluctance to leave.

Steine House

AMOROUS APPARITION

Many ghost stories involve accounts of awesome spectres and troublesome poltergeists that strike terror and fear into the hearts of those unfortunate enough to come upon them. In contrast to such formidable phenomena most spirits are thought to be quite benign; many even appear quite friendly - some perhaps a bit too friendly!

Black Lion Lane is an extremely narrow and gloomy little passage. It runs between Black Lion Street and Ship Street and is squeezed between two pubs; the Black Lion and the Cricketers. Midway down the passage are three old cottages thought to be some of the oldest remaining buildings in Brighton. Some sources claim they date from as early as the mid-sixteenth century. Their outward appearance, however, does not offer much evidence of this, possibly due to their facades having been altered down the years.

Ladies attending the Ghost Walk of the Lanes are repeatedly warned that one of the cottages is haunted by a particularly amorous apparition. His ethereal embraces have been felt by many women. By all accounts his insatiable urges have not diminished since his passing over; if anything he is thought to be more active now than when living!

Of all the haunted sites in and around the Lanes this narrow twitten seems the most foreboding. The little cottages sit silent and alone beneath the shadow of a high facing flint wall. On entering the passage one is immediately consumed with a sense of urgency and a need to scurry from the oppressiveness that hangs about the place. As all three cottages are privately owned it would be impertinent to disclose which one is deemed to be haunted. Nevertheless, those more attuned the supernatural might easily sense a paranormal energy emanating from the haunted one when passing by.

The ghostly goings on were first reported some years back by a former owner and lady artist whilst entertaining a friend. Her friend felt nothing sinister about the place and, after a pleasant evening with her host, retired to her room and soon fell into a blissful sleep. During the night, however, she awoke feeling curiously disorientated; her room appeared to be rocking. Then, to her horror, she realised it was her bed that was shaking. Now fully conscious the young woman sat up and clutching the bed

sheets, which were suddenly torn from her grasp. Fear held her in its grip and although wishing to flee the room felt herself restrained by an oppressive weight bearing down on her and of something breathing heavily into her face.

Although such boisterous phenomena must have been unsettling for the poor woman, it would seem mere paranormal trivia compared to what occurred later that same year when a lady visitor from France came to stay.

Cottages in Black Lion Lane; a dark and narrow little twitten. One of the buildings plays host to a particularly amorous apparition.

Like the previous guest the mademoiselle felt nothing threatening about the cottage and was looking forward to her stop-over in Brighton's most celebrated quarter - her mood was about to change! After retiring to her room she soon fell asleep but, as with the previous guest, awoke during the night feeling anxious and ill at ease. She then began to hear the incoherent mumblings of a man's voice. The sounds seemed to be coming from the room directly beneath hers. The mumblings were then replaced by the dull thud of lumbering footsteps ascending the stairs. The terrified mademoiselle sat up in bed rigid with fear, her eyes fixed firmly on the door. The footsteps paused momentarily on the landing before entering her room, bringing with them an extreme drop in temperature. She suddenly began to notice how one side of her bed had started to sag, as if someone was stretching out beside her. Then, to her horror, felt the cold chill of spectral hands begin caressing her. The marauding spectre's frosty fingers continued to fondle her trembling body for some moments. Finally, mustering all her strength, the mademoiselle managed to tear herself from the entity's clutches, leapt from the bed and switched on the light. Warm air had begun to fill the room; her spectral bedfellow had gone.

Despite all these shocking goings-on this amorous apparition never once tried to molest the lady of the house, who claimed to be a bit psychic. Maybe he thought that if he tried putting his grubby spectral mitts on her she would exorcise his spirit; so he kept them to himself. However, she did always feel the house had once belonged to an old sea captain. She would often sense him entering her sitting room and making himself comfortable in an old arm chair, which, for some inexplicable reason, would start

to creak as if someone was settling into it. Well, ladies, you know what sailors are!

Cottages in Black Lion Lane.

MEETING HOUSE PHANTOMS

The Friends' Meeting House in Prince Albert Street dates from 1805. It was originally a rather modest establishment until further extensions were added in 1875. It was built on land that once belonged to the Prior of St. Bartholomew. The gardens were originally a Quaker burial ground where some 54 adults and 34 children were placed in unmarked graves.

Enter the gardens and you might sense a strange, muted eeriness about the place. Those more attuned to the paranormal have frequently felt ill at ease while approaching the building. Peer through the heavy wrought iron gates in the shadowy twilight and you will understand why. An overwhelming sadness seems to emanate from the place. There have certainly been many reports of unexplained sightings and strange goings-on in the building down the years.

The rear wall to the building has long been associated with the spirit of Brighton's famous wandering nun.

The rear gate in Meeting House Lane leading to the Friends' Meeting House. The fleeting apparition of a small child in Victorian attire was witnessed sitting on the doorstep.

The Friends' Meeting House in Prince Albert Street where the sounds of lumbering footsteps and the rattling of keys has been heard.

Revisionists, however, have claimed that the apparition is more likely to be that of a Quaker woman whose plain, nineteenth century costume could easily be mistaken for a nun's cowl. Certainly the figure of a grey haired woman has been seen about the building. Some years ago a former warden witnessed the vague figure of a grey haired woman walking about late one night in the cottage where he lived. On entering the place he found no one there.

One evening a choir had been practising in the Meeting House. Following their rehearsal several members of the choir approached the warden to ask who the grey haired lady was who had been watching them. The warden was startled to hear this as the doors to the building had been locked for the duration of rehearsal and there was no one else in the building. More recently, the current warden, Terry Byrne, was on his own one evening and was convinced he had seen a grey haired lady going up the stairs. He went to investigate but, on searching the upper floor to the building, again found no one there.

The figure of a little girl, dressed in nineteenth century attire, has also been seen in the grounds of the Friends' Meeting House. She made a fleeting appearance perched on the steps to the rear of the building in Meeting House Lane. A local man, who claimed to have had several paranormal experiences in his lifetime, caught a brief glimpse of her one evening in the spring of 2009. Whilst walking past the back gate he saw a little girl of around three years of age sitting quietly on the doorstep. Glancing back, he noted that the child had gone. The man's double-take had been so swift it would not have afforded her time enough to scamper off. Interesting, in the same vicinity in

1997, a little girl of around the same age was seen in the basement of a shop called Bears and Friends in Meeting House Lane. The child was said to be of unkempt appearance and sitting on the lower steps of the stairs. A customer was quite taken by the child and was about to speak to her when she simply vanished.

Nevertheless, the most famous account of ghostly activity occurred when two young ladies, attending an evening class, found themselves locked inside the building. The incident occurred one evening in 1997. Following their class the ladies went to use the toilets. When they came to leave they noticed the place was in darkness and the doors locked. They sat at the foot of the stairs and made several attempts to contact their lecturer on their mobile phone, but received no reply. The girls then left a recorded message and waited in the hope that he might soon pick up on it. They sat, in the semi-darkness, at the foot of the staircase, pondering who to else they might call should they fail to get a response. The hollowness of the empty building seemed to echo their every move, causing them to feel particularly ill at ease. Nevertheless, they settled themselves down at the foot of the stairs and waited for their phone to ring. They were about to make another attempt to phone their lecturer when they were surprised to hear the sound of keys turning in a lock. An overwhelming sense of relief swept over them. They assumed it was the warden doing his rounds and got up to greet him. The sound of keys was heard once more, then a prolonged and uncomfortable silence. Suddenly posters and notes, which were pinned to a notice board, began to flutter as if someone was brushing past. Confusion then turned to fear causing the two ladies to huddle close and comfort each other.

Eventually one of the women managed to contact a relative who, in turn, called the police. Finally, a key holder was located and the two rather shaken ladies were released. Following their terrifying ordeal the two young women were cautious enough never to use the ladies facilities again following an evening lecture.

Rear courtyard at The Cricketers where the vague figure of a woman has been seen.

GHOST OF THE RIPPER

The Cricketers is thought to be one of the oldest pubs in Brighton; its cellars are said to date from as early as 1545. It was originally known as 'The Last and Fish Cart'; a 'last' being a term for 10,000 fish. The name changed in 1790 when a renowned Brighton cricketer became the landlord. During this time it was a boisterous hostelry frequented by fishermen who came to slake their angry thirsts in its rowdy saloon. Today the pub exudes a warm and genial ambience and is popular with townsfolk and tourists alike. It has also been a popular haunt for a many a local celebrity down the years. Graham Greene, the author, was particularly fond of the pub and is said to have written much of his crime novel, 'Brighton Rock', there. The upstairs bar has since been named 'The Greene Room' in his honour. Yet beneath the pub's convivial veneer, darker forces appear to be at work. There is much speculation that the pub once

The foot of the staircase in The Cricketers. Sounds of footsteps are often heard ascending the stairs to the upper floor landing. Orbs have been seen to appear in photographs taken in this area.

played host to one of this country's most notorious murderers, none other than Jack the Ripper!

Although the Ripper was never caught there are many theories as to his identity. However, it is widely believed he was one Robert D'Onston Stevenson, a former army surgeon, journalist and black magic practitioner. Ripperologist and author, Melvin Harris, firmly believed that Stevenson was unquestionably the notorious Whitechapel murderer, claiming: '...alone, of all the suspects, had the right profile of the opportunities, the motives, and the ideal cover. His background, his personality, his skills, his frame of mind, all [point to] him for the fateful role.' More interestingly there is evidence that Stevenson had resided at the Cricketers in 1888 when it was a lowly drinking den with cheap accommodation; possibly prior to committing those grisly murders in the gloomy backstreets of London's East End. Furthermore, it seemed that Stevenson was particularly fond of the place. Recurring paranormal activity at the pub might suggest his spirit is reluctant to leave. There have been many accounts of poltergeist activity occurring in the bar area, along with several appearances of a shadowy figure and sounds of lumbering footsteps about the place. If, indeed, this is the spirit of the Ripper, it is interesting to note that he commonly appears only to womenfolk.

A former landlady awoke one night to the clatter of barrels rolling around down in her cellars. Very nervously she made her way down to the cellar area. As she reached for the door handle the sounds ceased. On entering the place she discovered all the kegs to be perfectly aligned with plugs and pipes firmly attached. Some while later she started to become acutely aware of a sinister presence about the place, particularly whilst alone at night cleaning the bar. She would often experience the unsettling feeling of someone watching over her.

A few years later another couple came to manage the pub. Interestingly it was, once again, the landlady who became aware of the entity's presence. She claimed to have witnessed it on three separate occasions; once in the bar area and on two other occasions ascending the stairs. She described the spectre as always wearing a

The Ripper Room at The Cricketers. The walls are lined with information on the infamous Whitechapel murder of 1888. A key suspect was Robert D'Onston Stephenson, a former army surgeon, who lodged at The Cricketers.

long coat and wide-brimmed hat pulled low across its face, which she described as being indistinct and deathly pale apart from two horrible glaring eyes.

Could this have been the manifestation of the Ripper? Recent evidence seems to suggest perhaps it could. One night, as the pub was closing, a lady customer went the use the toilets; moments later she ran screaming from the place. After being consoled by the landlord she started to explain how, on entering the toilet, she had felt a presence; though

The Cricketers

she knew herself to have been alone. She went on to describe how she had then noticed a sudden drop in temperature seemingly enter the toilet cubicle. Then, to her horror, had felt the cold chill of spectral hands begin clawing at her face.

Quite often paranormal activity can cease as swiftly as it begins; although that does not appear to be the case as far as the Cricketers is concerned. If anything, the paranormal goings-on seem to have increased. The most common reoccurring phenomenon appears to be the recurrent sounds of footsteps ascending the starts to the upper floor. The pubs current Landlord, Kauser Ali, explained: "I will often hear the sound of footsteps ascending the stairs. For some reason they always stop outside my bedroom on the top floor. Although I've now grown used to it, my wife continues to feel very uncomfortable on that floor and there are certain rooms she will not enter."

This would certainly fit in with previous accounts of a shadowy figure being seen ascending the stairs to the upper floors. Furthermore, instances of unexplained occurrences have been reported in the upstairs bar area. One night after closing time, a former restaurant manager went around to every table blowing out the candles. When he returned to where he had begun, to his amazement, every single candle was once again alight. A young barmaid, also alone one night in the same area, found herself overcome with shock. Whilst clearing the tables overlooking the street, a window suddenly slammed violently shut. The terrified barmaid was so startled she ran screaming from the place.

Although Kauser remains unperturbed by the unexplained goings on in the pub it is his wife, as with previous landladies, that feels the most uncomfortable about the place. He also explained how many items in the pub have frequently gone missing only to reappear, often weeks later, in some other part of the building. "I have often put down various things, knowing full well where I have left them then, when I've returned, I've found them missing. They have the bizarre habit of turning up in another part of the pub; it's all very odd."

Several customers have also noted disturbing and unexplained occurrences about the place, particularly to the rear of the building and in the courtyard. The most recent phenomena appears to be that of the vague figure of a woman who is seen to walk the short distance between the toilets and the stockroom at the back of the pub; who she is, why she does this, and to what purpose, remains a mystery. One thing is certain; her appearance seems completely incongruent with all previous sightings of the alleged shadowy figure of the Ripper in his long cloak and wide-brimmed hat.

Digital photography has opened a whole new window into psychic research for, unlike film, digital cameras seem more able to capture orbs. These are small balls of light often thought to be spirits or paranormal energies. Several orbs have appeared in photographs taken around the downstairs bar area in the pub, particularly close to the foot of the staircase where the spirit of the Ripper is alleged to ascend. Moreover, many orbs have appeared it photographs taken by those attending the Ghost Walk of the Lanes when visiting the various haunted sites.

Anyway, old Jack is now beyond the reach of mortal law and harassment. However, ladies using the pub's facilities are advised to do so at their own risk!

OLD STRIKE-A-LIGHT

In the mid-eighteenth century Brighton, or Brighthelmstone as it was then known, was little more than a fishing village with a population of just 2000. The earliest fishing settlement was a mere humble assortment of dwellings strewn along the foreshore below the cliff and high water mark. These were mostly destroyed in the early part of that century by high tides and severe storms. It was on such a night that one of Brighton's most famous apparitions was to make its final dramatic appearance.

A relentless storm raged in the Channel, floundering through the waters like a wild serpent. Boats spun helplessly about in the swirling waves as fraught sailors struggled to bring their boats ashore. The skipper of one such vessel was a local fisherman named Swan Jervoise. He had known many a blustery night at sea, yet had never encountered one such as this. The mounting waves caused him to fear the worst yet, with dogged determination, stood steadfastly at the helm of his vessel, somehow managing to keep her on an even keel.

Although within just a mile of the shore the situation looked hopeless; huge waves pounded the deck and driving rain blurred visibility. The vessel's mainsail had been reduced to nothing more than forlorn rags that flapped helplessly in the ferocious wind. It seemed only a matter of time before the storm-battered boat would be drawn helplessly into the foaming vortex. Hope then suddenly shone upon Jervoise and his beleaguered crew. The welcoming glow of the town fire basket, a huge brazier ignited with fuel, used for guiding ships safely into port, could be seen through the driving sheets of rain.

Buffeted by the huge waves, Jervoise struggled desperately to keep the floundering rags of the boat's mainsail on a leeward tack. Then, as safety drew near, the little vessel was unexpectedly hoisted high atop the crest of a mountainous breaker and flung headlong towards the shore. Sounds of splitting timber and roaring surf rent the air as the boat became scuppered broadside against a bank of cobbles. As the crumbling vessel began to keel over the shaken crew leapt for their lives. Moments after scrabbling ashore the bedraggled men watched helplessly as the tidal undertow sucked the boat back into the foaming mouth of the angry waters.

As the men sat wearily mulling over their ordeal, Jervoise became distracted by curious flashes of light bursting from the slumbering darkness of the town. He then realised the dazzling lights appeared to be coming from the direction of the Rising Sun Inn, a place he knew well. The tavern sat at the southern end of East Street and was a rather lowly hostelry frequented by rowdy fishermen. Its cellars were often awash with seawater following high tides and from seepage off the Wellsbourne River, which, at that time, ran through the Old Steine. This perpetual leaching has caused huge stalactites to form in the cellars, which had come to resemble a dank and infested cavern. There had been terrible stories about this place and how it was haunted by a hideous, giant spectre known as Old-Strike-a-Light. He was claimed to be more creature than man, standing some seven feet in height and of awesome appearance. Many of the barmen had said they had seen him sitting aside a beer barrel down in the cellar wearing a bizarre conical hat whilst, all the while, jingling a gold coin in a pewter dish. Jervoise had always been amused by this, considering it to be mere fanciful bar talk from those with an over-active imagination.

Although exhausted from his ordeal, the drained and dishevelled fisherman set out to investigate. As he dragged himself wearily towards the tavern he was alerted by some rather curious scraping noises coming from within. It sounded like the striking of flints and he immediately wondered why anyone would be attempting to spark a fire at such a late hour. He was about to peer through the windows when he found himself literally thrown from his feet by a dazzling burst of light coming from the inn's windows. As he began scrabbling to his feet the doors of the tavern were suddenly flung open to reveal the colossal silhouette of a man. The monstrous form stood motionless, towering menacingly above the terrified fisherman. Jervoise then realised the tales of Old-Strike-a-Light had not been fanciful bar talk after all. The frightened fisherman fell to his knees as a cold tremor of fear drained what little strength he still had left. Then, with a slow, lumbering gait, the creature began making its way towards him. At which point, Jervoise screamed out in terror. In that instant, the hulking beast suddenly turned away and stumbled off into the night.

Picking himself up, Jervoise made for the safety of the inn. At which moment the innkeeper, having been awaked by all the commotion, arrived at the inn door with a lantern. Seeing the terrified looking fellow stumbling aimlessly in the street he began ushering him inside. He immediately tried to determine what was wrong, but could make no sense of the man's ramblings. Then, pacifying him as best he could, sat the trembling fisherman beside the glowing embers of the fire before going off to fetch a blanket. As he was leaving the bar the innkeeper was suddenly brought to a troubled halt on hearing Jervoise begin mumbling the words; Old-Strike-a-Light.

Consumed by visions of the creature, Jervoise then went into a frenzy and was about to flee the place. Just as he made for the inn door, however, he found the hulking entity had returned and now stood blocking his exit. The creature glared menacingly at Jervoise then, raising one arm, pointed a wavering finger towards the hearthstone. Overcome with fear, the frail and terrified fisherman fell into a faint.

On his return the innkeeper discovered Jervoise convulsing on the floor. He quickly wrapped him in a blanket and propped him in a chair beside the fire. The fisherman suddenly became delirious, jabbering frantically about the colossal spectre that had pursued him. Showing concern for the man's frail and tortured state the innkeeper sent his wife to fetch Father Anselm from the nearby Priory of St. Bartholomew. The kindly priest listened intently as Jervoise continued to stammer obsessively about the events that had befallen him. In the following minutes he became hysterical, haunted by the menacing vision of the spectre. His eyes began to bulge manically from their sockets and, venting a cry of unimaginable horror, froze transfixed in the agony of death as the life blood drained from him.

Sometime later both the innkeeper and Father Anselm reflected on where the spectre had been pointing. They seemed to agree that perhaps his appearance had not been to terrify the living but, moreover, to alert them to something of importance. They therefore decided to remove the old hearthstones. To their astonishment an old oak casket was discovered, crammed with Spanish doubloons. From that day onward no more was seen or heard of Old-Strike-a- Light. It seemed he was at last at peace having alerted the living to his hidden cache.

THE DRUID'S HEAD

The Druid's Head is thought to be one of the oldest taverns in Brighton. The original structure is said to date from around 1510, but was possibly a private house until it acquired a beer license in 1830. It has certainly played host to all manner of unexplained goings-on down the years and is perhaps haunted by several apparitions from different periods in time. The pub is so named after a ring of stones, believed to be associated with Druidic rituals, which were located nearby some two hundred years ago.

The Druids were a priestly civilisation originating in Gaul who indulged in many barbaric rites. Roman writers often discussed the Druid's practise of human sacrifice, which

The Bar at the Druid's Head. Glasses have been seen to move along its surface unaided.

was outlawed by the Emperor Tiberius. Due to the number of unexplained goings-on in the pub, one is drawn to wonder whether it could be associated with the troubled souls of sacrificial victims. There has certainly been much of the poltergeist activity witnessed at the pub. One

Flagstone plaque in the entrance to the bar at the Druid's Head.

particular incident, which occurred in the early 1990's, could add some validity to this theory.

Contrary to popular belief that ghosts only appear at night, many seem to appear during the daylight hours, as was discovered by a young barmaid named Cindy Wilkinson. Whilst attending the lunchtime trade she could not help but notice a woman in a long red dress standing in close proximity to the person she was serving.

Although she found nothing unusual in her attire, the barmaid was particularly taken by her pallid complexion and of the glazed and distant look in her eyes. She asked another member of the bar staff if they would serve her; at which point, the woman in red simply vanished. So fleeting was the apparition it was difficult for the young barmaid to discern whether or not she had been wearing a red dress; or could it have been a blood-stained sacrificial gown?

In the early 1960's the pub was beginning to look rather jaded and extensive refurbishment was undertaken. Whilst the building work was being carried out two old tunnels were discovered leading from the cellars. One led in the direction of the sea and had possibly been used by smugglers at one time or another; the other ran in the direction of the Royal Pavilion. Many feel it was used by the Prince Regent for smuggling in ladies of dubious repute. A man is said to have met a brutal death in one of the tunnels. One theory is that he was a smuggler bludgeoned by customs and excise men. There are those who firmly believe it is his troubled spirit that tries to gain contact with the living. If indeed it is his spirit, he has been known to become quite boisterous. Glasses and bottles have been seen to shift around on shelves and glasses move unaided along the bar surface. Lights have also been known to flicker unaccountably, although the electrical connections have been checked for faults on numerous occasions.

There is a common belief that, for some reason, children are more attuned to paranormal activity. In fact it is not uncommon to hear instances of children having seen and, in some cases, verbally communicated with deceased relatives. Interestingly, all three young daughters of former tenant, Les Walker, claimed to have had paranormal encounters at the pub. One daughter frequently spoke of seeing 'funny men' enter her little

Steps leading to the cellar where a hooded figure was seen.

The cellar of the Druid's Head. A hooded figure was seen to disappear beneath the stairs.

attic room. The two other daughters also said they had seen a ghost about the place. One of the girls maintained she had heard it call out her name. Mr. Walker was also convinced of having seen an apparition in the pub as was Derek Woods, who managed the pub in the 1970's. Mr. Wood's experience was a very common one, as paranormal encounters go, in that it was quite transitory. The incident occurred one night down in the cellars. Woods claimed to see, for a 'flitting instant', a hooded figure dart beneath the staircase close to the blocked-up tunnel where the brutal murder is thought to have taken place.

Many rumours still abound regarding ghostly goings-on at the pub. Furthermore, various members of bar staff claim to have felt uncomfortable about the place, particularly

The Druid's Head.

down in the cellar area. Hardly surprising as there have now been around a hundred sightings of ghosts and associated phenomena there. In an interview with the Brighton Argus the current bar manager, Yvonne Roache, said: "I prefer to ignore the ghost stories. I don't like thinking about it because I live above the pub." Presumably Yvonne does not venture into the little attic room too often, nor go down into the cellars to change the barrels!

HIDEOUS SPECTRE OF OLD STEINE

For many years the Old Steine was a barren, muddy area of common land close to the old town used by the fishing community. It was a place where fishermen could repair their boats, dry nets and cure fish. The Wellesbourne, considered to Brighton's 'lost river', ran down the west side until it was eventually channelled through vast Victorian sewers. In the late eighteenth century the Steine became a fashionable area for the upper classes to promenade about its freshly lain gravel paths. However, it is a place where is said to lurk one of Brighton's most horrific apparitions, widely believed to be spirit of the onetime adventurer and soldier of fortune, John Robinson.

Steine or Old Steine where the horrific apparition of John Robinson has been seen to appear.

Robinson was, by all accounts, a refined and well-educated man who bore a remarkable resemblance to that dashing character of popular fiction, Sir Percy Blakeney; otherwise known as the Scarlet Pimpernel. The 'Pimpernel' was a character created by Baroness Emma Orczy, whose heroic adventures during the French Revolution captured the public's imagination. Like his fictional counterpart, Robinson also abhorred the revolution and set about rescuing many beleaguered French noblemen. Whilst smuggling a whole family to safety he found himself caught in an affray and, in the process, killed three members of the Revolutionary Guard. He soon became a wanted man with a high price on his head. Nevertheless, Robinson was an astute and resourceful man who was able to evade capture and somehow make his way back to England.

Following his exploits during the French Revolution he travelled to Persia, where, as a mercenary soldier, became involved in a civil war. Unfortunately, he backed the wrong

Steine.

side and was captured by the victorious Agfa Muhammad. In a brutal act of vengeance, Agfa is said to have demanded twenty thousand pairs of eyes. Robinson, along with several thousand other rebels, was subjected to the most horrendous torture, which culminated in him having his eyes burned out with hot irons. He was subsequently thrown onto the streets of Tehran to become a beggar. This once proud and dignified man was now reduced to a lowly and pitiful existence. Then, by chance, in 1799, he was found by a kindly English merchant who took pity on him and brought him home to England. Somehow Robinson made his way back to Brighton, where he laid down on the Old Steine and died before an inquisitive group of onlookers. Those who saw him stood aghast at the sight of his horrifically mutilated face which, it is claimed, had maggots feasting on the putrefying flesh.

His appearance clearly caused quite a stir and several alarming accounts captured the imagination of a local wordsmith who penned a rhyme in his honour, which read:

> *"Don't ye dally, darling dear, in Brighton's city clear.*
> *The ghost of old John Robinson is waiting for ye there.*
> *If ye look into his face, you'll end your days that night.*
> *For he'll steal your eyes from you to give a beggar sight."*

As the years passed sightings of Robinson's mutilated form became less frequent until he became almost forgotten. Then, for some inexplicable reason, his grisly appearance seemed to be reawakened. This occurred on one rather grim night in 1957. A police officer, while on his beat, saw the figure of a man lying close to the gutter alongside the Old Steine. He thought at first it was a drunk who had taken a fall. Fearing for the man's safety the officer strode across the road to assist him. As he stooped to take hold of the fellow he caught sight of his face; although it could hardly be described as such. A festering mask of decomposing flesh confronted the officer. He later described it as being hideous beyond belief with two dark, weeping sockets where its eyes should have been. Repulsed by what he had seen the officer become physically sick. On recovering he was astounded to discover the horribly mutilated man had disappeared.

Robinson's abhorrent form was to make yet another dramatic appearance a short while after. Following an evening performance at the Theatre Royal, a lady theatre-goer was making her way home across the Old Steine. She decided to sit for a moment on a bench to take the night air. Suddenly, as if from nowhere, Robinson's awesome form manifested itself directly in front of where the woman sat. His repugnant, decaying face, with its awesome, lifeless sockets, glared menacingly at the terrified woman. Letting out a scream, she fell into a faint only to awake some time later in the Royal Sussex Hospital, where she remained overnight in order to recover from her shock.

To this day there have been many official and unofficial reports of Robinson's mutilated form lumbering blindly about the Old Steine. However, since Brighton now hosts an annual Zombie Walk, with a Beach of the Dead after party, one could incur some difficulty in spotting him.

TOWN HALL GHOSTS

THE PHANTOM FRIAR

Brighton Town Hall is an imposing structure built in the neoclassical style with Doric and Ionic columns. The building dates from 1830 and stands close to the former Priory of St Bartholomew, which was destroyed in a raid by the French in 1514. When excavation work was carried out, to the west of the building, many old walls were discovered along with some skeletal remains; quite possibly those of monks. It is hardly surprising therefore that a phantom friar has been seen in the cellars and places nearby. His alarming appearance has been witnessed on several of occasions.

Legend has it that a former brother from the Priory committed a serious offence that undermined his religious status. Some say he was found in a state of inebriation having consumed copious amounts of communion wine. Whatever his crime there would have been little tolerance shown by the elders of a priory in those days. Any indiscretion that discredited the sacred order would have been dealt with promptly and in a most draconian manner. After much deliberation it was agreed he should be excommunicated to become shamed and destitute.

Apart from this fleeting indiscretion the poor fellow had no doubt lived a devout life, going about his business in a most exemplary manner. It is possible therefore that he still retains a sense of belonging to the priory. Mediums often believe that nuns and monks continue their spiritual work in the afterlife as guardians of the living. There have certainly been similar sightings at other religious sites around the country. Perhaps he never came to terms with his expulsion and returns in the forlorn hope of forgiveness. This would certainly concur with the theory that many spirits seem to linger in this life because they remain troubled or have some unfinished business to attend to.

Apart from his many appearances at the Town Hall he has been seen elsewhere in and around the Lanes, from a graveyard in Queen's Road to the Royal Pavilion Gardens. However, the most dramatic sighting was at a stationer's shop in East Street during the 1950's. A young lady sales assistant and her manageress were working late in a room above the shop sorting through a consignment of diaries. Suddenly realising she had left her list downstairs; the young assistant went to fetch it. Moments later the manageress heard her ascending the stairs, but was puzzled by her rather slow, lumbering gait. Turning around, she was horrified to find herself face to face with the phantom friar. Although that was not altogether true, for there was no head inside his hood...only darkness! The poor woman was too breathless with fear to even scream; she simply turned on her heels and fled downstairs.

There has been little evidence of our bedraggled friar in recent years. Perhaps he has at last found peace, or gained forgiveness, and no longer wanders the shadowy netherworld twixt this life and the next.

THE HARRIDAN ON THE STAIRS

Possibly the most disturbing entity in the Town Hall is that of a repulsive hag-like creature. She is said to be hideous beyond belief, dressed in a long, voluminous black dress and a conical hat on her head similar to a witch of folklore. At least one Town Hall employee had the misfortune of actually seeing her materialize while ascending the interior staircase.

Many council employees have sensed her presence. Others have complained of feeling a sudden unearthly chill pass through them. More disturbing are those who have actually experienced her long, flowing gown brush past them. Nevertheless, such incidents seem trivial compared to what happened to a lady cleaner unfortunate enough to find herself alone one night in that part of the building.

While cleaning the stairs the woman began to sense someone glaring at her. The feeling then became increasingly intense; at which point she decided to pack away her cleaning things and leave. In that instant, the feeling suddenly became quite overwhelming. She was about to leave when, to her horror, a sickening witch-like creature began to materialise before her very eyes. The terrified

The central staircase, Brighton Town Hall, where a hideous hag-like creature has been seen to appear.

Brighton Old Town Hall built in 1830. The building is said to house three apparitions.

woman stood for a moment quaking with fear from the look of bitter hatred on the hag's face. Then, stumbling down the staircase, the poor woman took refuge beneath a table at the foot of the stairs. There she remained, huddled and trembling, until discovered sometime later by another employee.

Why this loathsome creature persists in manifesting itself, or to what purpose, remains a mystery. Nevertheless, one thing is certain; she seems consumed with a bitter hatred and continues to strike terror and fear into the hearts of all who come upon her.

'ORRIBLE MURDER

The Town Hall holds claim to a unique and sinister crime, which occurred during the mid-nineteenth century. On the night of March 13th, 1844, a most gruesome murder took place in its cellars. The victim was Henry Solomon, Brighton's Chief Constable, and the only Chief Officer in British history to have been murdered whilst on duty.

In those days the Town Hall cellars were occupied by the local constabulary; all manner of rogues were brought in and locked-up in their rather gloomy old cells. On this occasion a local villain by the name of John Lawrence had been hauled in for questioning. Lawrence was well known with the local Bobbies. His nefarious activities had prompted frequent interrogations by police officers. By all accounts he had taken part in a robbery at a local furniture store from which a carpet had been stolen. He was subsequently brought in for questioning and led down into the cells where he found himself confronted by the Chief Constable.

Solomon plied him with questions, but received little response. Moreover, Lawrence became increasingly agitated and uncooperative. Rather exasperated by the man's lack of cooperation, Solomon told him to take a seat beside the fireplace until further required. In so doing he made a fatal mistake; a mistake that would cost him his life! For one brief moment he turned his back on Lawrence. In that fleeting instant, Lawrence leapt from his chair and took hold of a heavy iron poker from the hearth. Before Solomon realised what was happening, Lawrence was upon him administering a frenzied attack. A series of lethal blows dashed the Chief Constable's brains out. Lawrence was subsequently convicted of murder at Lewes Assizes and later hanged outside of Horsham jail.

The fireplace in the old police cells, Brighton Town Hall, where Solomon suffered a brutal attack.

Since then the spectral figure of a man, clad in dark attire, has been seen down in the cellars. In the 1980's a security guard, while on duty, was awe-struck to see the apparition of a man in a long, dark coat and top hat appear from the area of the old cells. Such distinguishing Victorian attire could well suggest this was, indeed, the troubled spirit of the murdered Chief Constable.